PRAISE FOR SKYROCKET DIVE

"Long before most of us conjured our first moon/June couplet, Fred Poole, in such bold and abrasive books as *Where Dragons Dwell* (Harpers, 1971) and the exposé *Revolution in the Philippines: the U.S. in a Hall of Cracked Mirrors* (McGraw-Hill, 1984) put it down on the page the way it was meant to be: gangster, defiant, unapologetic. So it comes as no surprise that *Skyrocket Dive*, Poole's first full-length collection of poems, proudly and loudly published by CAPS Press, continues a long legacy of truth seeking and truth telling.

Like dispatches from an eroding front line, be that line political, national, global, health oriented or environmental, Poole's power to pull you away from the allure of the shiny new objects they create to ensnare and enslave rings like a hall of trumpets throughout *Skyrocket Dive*. How we always see things through the geography of childhood no matter our stance on the evolutionary scale. As his insight sharpens despite age, he finds himself (thereby alerting the rest of us) that "even more I dream without any certainty." *Skyrocket Dive* is Fred Poole once more mounting the barricades, calling us all to rise up with him."
— *Mike Jurkovic,* author
mooncussers (Luchador Press 2022) and *AmericanMental* (Luchador Press 2020)
President, Calling All Poets, Hudson Valley, NY

"This book of poems reflects the life of a man who has taken the tyranny of uncertainty in life (which drives most people crazy) and transformed it into a sublime form. His words manifest what courage is when actually lived and portrayed through poetic form."
— *Chris Collins,* social justice poet

"Do you ARTFULLY want to know and FEEL LIFE? Even when life elicits WHAT??? I guarantee that Fred Poole will lead your heart to a garden of TRUTH."
— *Linda Mary Montano,* Performance Artist

"Fred's profound dignity and gentleness makes his raw, emotional truths all the more moving and powerful."
— *Greg Correll,* writer and editor
CUNY Writers Institute 2017

"In the two decades in which I've been a CAPS fan, I have been wowed time and again by the poets and the poetry of my beloved Hudson Valley. What you hold in your hands is but the tip of a glorious iceberg, but what a refreshing tip it is!"
— *John Leonard Pielmeier,* actor, poet, playwright *(Agnes of God, The Boys of Winter, Hook's Tale, The Exorcist)* novelist, *(Hook's Tale)*; screenwriter *(The Pillars of The Earth)*

"This anthology captures the vital community of writers living in the Hudson Valley. Calling All Poets over the course of twenty years as evidenced in this volume has nurtured and supported numerous poets, with distinct voices, approaches, styles, and genres. This is a rich and compelling collection of works that speaks deeply to many aspects of the human experience and provides illumination; childhood memories, family relationships, lost love, the search for the meaning in existence, and the witnessing of injustice are all powerfully portrayed. I appreciate the range of form and style from lyric poems to personal and prose poetry , from rich descriptive sensory pieces to philosophical inquiries and surreal and mythic visions. This is a volume that deserves to be read many times, and each time a reader will find new poetic treasures."
— *Jan Zlotnik Schmidt,* SUNY Distinguished Teaching Professor co-editor of *A Slant of Light: Contemporary Women Writers of the Hudson Valley*

"Calling All Poets has successfully created a diverse community of poets and writers who support one another. Whenever I'm there, I feel as if I am part of something bigger, a movement in the arts. In addition, they have embraced technology, streaming readers outside the area live and broadcasting the events online. Calling all Poets is the best series in the Hudson Valley!"
— *Rebecca Schumejda,* poet *Cadillac Men, Waiting at the Dead End Diner*

"CAPS is about poetry of course. But it's also about community, how it's actually created a community of diverse personalities and backgrounds that come together each month to speak in the one language we all know: The spoken word. Every month there's a mark on the calendar that we all look forward to."
— *Ken Holland,* poet, Pushcart nominee

"The Hudson Valley boasts a plethora of fascinating poets whose active participation in readings and local events makes them a reliable source of wisdom and inspiration."
— *Dr. Lucia Cherciu,* poet *Lepdarea de Limb (The Abandonment of Language)*

"The Hudson Valley gives voice to writers and poets who have something of value to say and a comfortable environment for accomplishing this important endeavor. From the caves of Rosendale to the richness of Roost Studios, the Hudson Valley has nurtured me and advanced my career."

— *Eddie Bell,* author, poet
Capt's Dreaming Chair, Festival of Tears

"The Hudson Valley is one of the most vibrant and exciting poetry regions in the country and Calling All Poets at in Beacon is a centerpiece for the power of words. I feel fortunate to be part of this creative current and to be able to share the art of language with the hundreds of writers I've met and whose works I've been able to read and hear over the years."

— *Laurence Carr,* author
Pancake Hollow Primer; editor: *Reflecting Pool: Poets and the Creative Process* and *Riverine;* co-editor of *WaterWrites* and *A Slant of Light* (Codhill Press)

"Thanks to both the many hardworking poetry hosts and the scores of poets who come out to share their work it sometimes seems one could attend a reading every day. And the truly wonderful thing is that the region is home to a number of extremely gifted poets who can leave an audience wishing their reading would never end."

— *Matthew J. Spireng,* poet, and three time Pushcart nominee

"I can't imagine living anywhere else in the world. Where else could I find the variety, the devotion, the matter-of-fact respect for poetry not just as an art but a fact of life? From the poetry gangs of Albany to the lost souls of Orange County, I believe the Hudson Valley provides a unique climate for poets of all inclinations to share their work in a supportive environment, a gift not always available to other creators."

— *Cheryl A. Rice,* poet
My Minnesota Boyhood, Moses Parts The Tulips

"Generations of painters have drawn inspiration from the age-worn corrugations in Hudson Valley landscapes and the glow of the skies overhead after late-summer thunderstorms give way to dusk. Folk singers impassioned by the rainbow taint of pollutants in the fabled Hudson River gave voice to the modern environmental movement. This latest collection of verse penned by the region's poets—from acidic to comedic to political to pastoral— shows how fertile the ground here is for the written and spoken word, as well. Dive in!"

— *Andy Revkin,* longtime environmental journalist, sometime songwriter

"The CAPS Anthology is living proof that poetry, literature and those who continue to create and/or appreciate it are not defined by their location, education, pigmentation or social station. In 2019, The Anthology's home base, the historic Hudson Valley, retains the same magical spirit that inspired 19th Century visual artists to excel and reflect their surroundings. After reading this new collection in the latest CAPS Anthology, we all look forward to MORE!!! Thank you Calling All Poets and all of today's poets for inspiring us and our kids by sharing words and images of lasting value!!"

— *David Amram,* conductor, composer
with Jack Kerouac, the undisputed co-founder of what has become *Jazzoetry*

"The twentieth anniversary Calling All Poets Anthology consists of some of the best poems by more than forty poets included in the CAPS poetry reading series. The collection is dedicated to Donald Lev (1936-2018) who edited and published Home Planet News, among countless contributions to the literary community. Among the mellifluous vein of talented poets, a sample includes Laurence Carr, Donald Lev, Susan Hoover, Mary Makofske, Roger Aplon, Irene O'Garden, Rebecca Schumejda, Matthew J. Spireng, Lucia Cherciu, Ruth Danon, Bertha Rogers, Jim Eve, Pauline Uchmanowicz, and Mike Jurkovic. This is an anthology that speaks to the current political climate, to nature and climate change, to family dynamics and all phases of human life. Whether shouts or celebrations, prayers or meditations, these poems demonstrate that the Hudson River a shelter for poets and dreamers today just as it once was for Hudson River School painters in the nineteenth century.

— *Margo Taft Stever*, author
Cracked Piano (CavanKerry Press, 2019)

"What if the poets of the Hudson Valley had a party and everybody came? This hospitable and yet lively (read: rockin') anthology catches that spirit. This isn't a Hudson River School of poetry. It's a Hudson Valley lyric line dance. Everyone's invited. Come on down."

— *TR Hummer*, poet
Eon (LSU Press, 2018), After The Afterlife (Acre Books, 2018),
The Infinity Sessions (Southern Messenger Poets, 2005)

"The varied crowd Calling All Poets attracts makes for lively nights. It's rare that we have a dull evening. The fact that the hosts are welcoming and gracious for the presence of a supportive crowd speaks volumes. You don't have nearly the sense of camaraderie anywhere else."

— *Christopher Wheeling,* poet, CAPS photographer

"I believe that if CAPS continues on the path it is now blazing it will become an important milestone in the growth of American Poetry."

— *Glenn Werner,* poet
Premeditated Contrition and other poems, CAPS Tech Czar

"Poets have grown up at CAPS."

— *Jim Eve,* poet,
founder, co-host, Calling All Poets

Skyrocket Dive

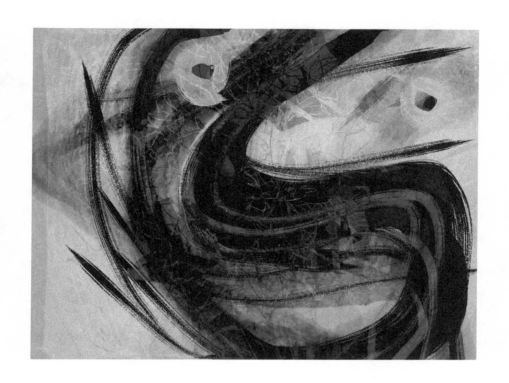

Skyrocket Dive

Fred Poole

CAPS
PRESS

With special thanks to Mike Jurkovic, Greg Correll, and Jim Eve of Calling All Poets —
known by its many friends as CAPS, a poetry community that began in the
Hudson Valley many years ago and which has now spread worldwide.
— Fred Poole

Calling All Poets, Inc (CAPS)
79 Sargent Ave Beacon NY 12508

callingallpoets.net

Ordering Information:

For details, contact info@callingallpoets.net.

Print ISBN: 978-0-9973258-6-7

eBook ISBN:

Printed in the United States of America

First Edition

Design, production, editing, and illustration credits:

Book design and production: small packages, inc
smallpackages.com

Cover Image: Greg Correll
gregcorrell.com

for Marta

Fred Poole's poetry does not rely on tricks to strike you right in the heart. But we have to meet him where he lives. He doesn't spare us, because he doesn't spare himself. He looks at his present state with clear eyes and reports on how he feels about it.

Age and infirmity have been slowly reducing his movement in the outside world, stealing away freedoms that he used to take for granted, as most of us do. His condition now keeps him stationary in a place that he didn't choose and where he'd rather not be. It could happen to any of us. He speaks to us directly.

He's not trying to teach us anything, for which I'm grateful. (There are so many wise and pretty posts on Facebook, and too many of these are platitudinous and useless.) He's doing something much more important. He's bearing witness to a life, to his life as he's living it now, to Life.

The work is classically elegiac, as it's about loss, about the death of certain beloved things, so it's profoundly sad.

As in:

> No, that is not my room.
>
> Not my very old shoes, and not my corduroy jacket.
>
> Not my boots for walking.
>
> Trying everywhere to combat cold and heat
>
> But snow and sun,
>
> Cold and hot,
>
> Are what I want back.
>
> These things I want again.

And this:

> Over and over I lose things,
>
> And pray for their reappearance
>
> Much like losing my way on
>
> A forest path
>
> Or in a city
>
> Or in what I thought of as home.

But the truth of his lived experience isn't limited to the somber. It's richer and more varied. There's anger. "It is taking a long time to get a Percocet"; or when he tells us that the invitation to join in some "fun and games" turns his stomach. There's often mordant humour: "Please God help me find my iPhone."

There's also acknowledgement of the world's beauty. When this light pierces through, we are relieved for Fred, and relieved for ourselves as we needed this.

> I have encountered a fox,
>
> And flocks of geese
>
> And flocks of wild turkeys
>
> And two displaced young coyotes.

And then, of course, he reminds us of the complicated truth with his last lines.

> I hear the two coyotes are still around watching
>
> Through a window to the room
>
> From where I look out
>
> On what is not mine.

Fred's poems are a rich offering. I'm grateful. Outside my rented flat, I see my cats curled in in a sunny spot on the veranda. Bombs are pummelling Kyiv. Fred is writing in the room he didn't choose and wondering about the lives of birds he sees out the window.

How are we to live? He shows us how he does it:

> Just when I am winning.
> I look at the painting
> Of Monet's houseboat
> And even more I dream
> Without any certainty.

To "dream without any certainty" is to embrace the actual alongside the possible, without hope and without despair. Fred embraces his experience with a love of beauty clarified by fearless honesty. We are very lucky to have him in this world.

> — *Sigrid Heath*
> Author of *A Far Cry*
> Paros, Greece

THE WORM SITUATION

Where are all the worms
And why are so few people
As concerned?
Spiders too.
But spiders have a supportive press
While no one googles Wonder Worm Woman.
When I was trying to be a fisherman
The third time around
It was what I was doing to the worms that got to me.

MINE NOT MINE

No, that is not my room.

Not my very old shoes, and not my corduroy jacket.

Not my boots for walking.

Trying everywhere to combat cold and heat

But snow and sun,

Cold and hot,

Are what I want back.

These things I want again.

No time for the sadness I feel

In this place not my room

This particular sadness overrun by anger.

For in this place I'm in

Words I hear every day are:

"Come on down for some fun and games"

Such words in the air in

Where I am what they call a resident,

The word "resident" sounding to me like "inmate"

I might be happy to think such words

Like the words fun and games,

Turn my stomach

And right now I want everyone

To be quiet with the Christmas things

Music and prayer

Which fill my ears or worse my heart.

This place.

Also the place where
Looking or moving out from where I moved,
I have encountered a fox,
And flocks of geese
And flocks of wild turkeys
And two displaced young coyotes.
I hear the two coyotes are still around watching
Through a window to the room
From where I look out
On what is not mine.

WHAT ABOUT LIVER?

Hot times tonight
Wearing white bucks
That are dirty
Which was the shoe style.
In the garden
Where I start
And eat everything
Except meat.
Which I do not miss, I say
Any more than I miss being
Pummeled by bullies.
But I miss dogs. Cats too.
And chipmunks.
Raw meat?
Raw burger?
Goat meat
Just as this goat is killed.
It is dark out already.
What about liver?
What about your berries
That twist the tongue?
People forget that even
Vegetable matter
Can be disgusting.

I remember without the need
For anything sickening
Though maybe sickening would
Help with undercooked fish
Or mixed with feces
Just when I am winning.
I look at the painting
Of Monet's houseboat
And even more I dream
Without any certainty.

FACEBOOK PRAYERS

I'm praying for you,
I sometimes say on Facebook
Not praying for myself
Which I almost never do,
Except here on Facebook,
Where I say,
"I do not want to die"
But I pray for more than that,
And I can be more specific,
As in "Please God help me
Find my iPhone"
Which is something I say
More than once in any day
While outside my window another snowfall
And birds seem to get bigger
I mean the big black ones
That are surely ravens.
Over and over I lose things,
And pray for their reappearance
Much like losing my way on
A forest path
Or in a city
Or in what I thought of as home.

REALLY DYING?

Is it because they think I am dying, is that why they are so nice to me?

Or is it because I have been beaten down mentally to the point of going along with niceness?

They prefer to call us "residents" instead of "patients"

I repeat that if I am not a patient but a resident, it seems they will always have me

In this strange anti-socialism American medical world.

Where almost the only decent part is that nurses tend to be smooth and attractive.

My greatest fear — I say not for the first time — is that with or without appealing nurses and attendants I could come to like this place

Still, there is some real kindness here. And that is the most dangerous part of all — the danger again of coming to like this place.

Not just having people who will clean you up if you have what they call here an accident — like the kind word used by a sympathetic parent or medical professional.

Of course if an appealing nurse or attendant cleans you up all is well from all directions

And beyond all that

The importance of the setting,

A place for fine sunsets

But there is a mandated lack of pets

And now there's all this baby talk

As if that will make adults feel better.

And all these people here with limited if any access to their minds.

PLUS DRINKING

I didn't drink or smoke in boarding school.

These were for the dumb jocks who were my enemies

Who tortured me when they could

Until through debating I brought in much bigger trophies than theirs

Their intrinsically mediocre sports victories.

Revenge this time being what it was cracked up to be.

And I had high hopes for alcohol.

Not so much the heavy drinking I saw at home as that which I read about in F. Scott Fitzgerald

His *The Great Gatsby*, I decided, would be my favorite book.

One day after my heavy drinking was underway I told everyone around me that we had a great night ahead.

I did not believe it even as the night in question unfolded.

I was bothered that a first drink of alcohol often made me sick.

My solution was to drink harder and faster,

Whatever I did now made me feel worse.

Later I learned to call it depression

TRANSITIONS

A beautiful bright woman with whom I had worked on writing suddenly
Sent me a text wishing me well in the "transition."
Is "transition" the same as saying "Have a nice death?"
People out of other places have been sending texts and emails saying what a writerly if not spiritual person I am.
It is taking a long time to get a Percocet
Because everyone is so busy
Here when not everyone is here.
Here in this stage of my transition.
It is not at all like what millions of Iraqis and Haitians and Afghans went through when they had transitions.
Unreal byways though it a metaphor for who knows what.
I want to stay up late partly because late nights are connected to being alive.
I would use the TV if that did not feel I would always be in an old folks home room.
Maybe I should tell people I am doing much needed work on Americans in old folks homes.

MAKING LIFE EASIER

Glimpse of a Cardinal
Glimpse of a Blue Jay
Head-on with birds with
Puffed up white breasts
White-breasted Nuthatches?
Then looking out a wide window
That I don't want to call my window.
Fearing again to mean I'll always be here
But when and how is not being here?
Maybe already too late
To not be here
Like too late to be a pilot again
Or someone who can play music.
Like too late to marry
Now is the time,
I would like to think,
When I can double back
And look again at
People, places and paintings
That I like to think
Were essential to my making my life.

When I was discovering poetry
And left/liberal politics
And decided I had to rid myself
Of what religion still did in my mind.
So much to get rid of
So much that was mundane
Like loyalty to a college
And professional sports
And religion might be
as mundane
As television dramas
If true this would make life easier.

A LITTLE SUICIDAL

I was roaming in the night. Not in Paris where I had been.
Nor Bangkok where I wanted to go
But roaming in these flat streets,
With their flatter air
All night though with a daytime job to go to.
Sometimes too hot or too cold, in Indianapolis.
Sometimes smelly from lack of breezes.
Or lack of culture, I might have said,
When I was making fun of the place,
From my position at 22 as someone from near New York
Who had just graduated without honors from Princeton
Hardly knowing yet how I hated Princeton.
But in my putting down of Indianapolis,
It was as if Princeton were a real credential
As my experience of it
Had filtered through my drunkenness.
And though I was not suicidal,
I felt the end of everything
As I roamed past a burlesque house.

And the movie theaters I frequented

The seedy old burlesque house

Was not for me the sign

Of another time

This reluctant virgin's chance

To see slinky and dubious

And therefore appealing

Naked women or girls,

And still it felt like I was walking through

What very likely could be

The end of everything

KILLING OR NOT

I watch birds for hours and do not know their breeds or many other of their names I can use.

From early on I suspected I could not know everything, bright and up to date as I was.

I received a blow job in Atlanta before I knew it could be done.

And this did not ruin me for life.

Any more than did my first French kiss, meaning kiss with tongues.

The difference was that the blow job took place in a whorehouse while the French kiss was on home ground.

It did not seem like a great difference.

While in my consciousness there was the vaguest connection between sex and death.

In case you want to beat me to death it is important you

know I am unarmed

But I believe in anger.

Just as I believe the whole story should always get out.

Which I say not just as a writer

As a lover of beauty and respecter of trauma too.

So I puzzle myself for not writing so far about contemplated suicide.

KILLING WITH CUTENESS

Being treated like a child

Infantile

Infanticide

Head heavy.

Where do I go from here?

Is there any place to go except

death?

I am tired of hearing that most old folks homes are worse.

It has been seventy years since anyone had the gall to call me by the cruel prep school nickname, "Speedy."

But now in this place some are trying the same thing with my other most hated nickname, "Freddy."

I was taken here against my will, another reminder of boarding school.

This time the bullies, disguised as young aides, are using the name Freddy to disparage what they consider old age.

Disparage it or nullify it with cuteness.

Unlike prep school this place has only a miserable little library.

Needed because no one who works here is ever seen with a book.

And as if to make it worse they have made it almost impossible for a patient to get into the little library. Because of "meetings."

And to make it worse still,

Many or most cannot understand why anyone would want to get in.

There is a very high level of dementia here.

But it is not the demented I am talking about.

OK I DO RESOLVE IN THE NEW YEAR

To insist on privacy here and everywhere
To go against them
By getting well
To go against them
By being mobile
To have sympathy with
Those whose brains are failing
People experiencing my greatest fear
My brain is working so
I can write and read
As I never have before
So I speak politically
Without stepping into shit
Though less so when face to face
If not so clear about death.
I would like to think I can
Face death bravely
While all around me are
People with dementia.
A problem, since I do not want
this place to turn out well for me
as I am productive here
Writing poetry
And sometimes sleep here despite
Radios playing church Latin
And mentally rough ranting
From those here who have it worst.

Not happy,

I will not admit to that

But I had many

Deathlike times when out from under

Such a place as this, I

Wishing for pure cool water

The feel of ferns

The sight of chipmunks

The smell of cactus

Wind blowing towards me

Sun burning hot in October

And birds everywhere

Even

when I look for them.

THE WRONG SORT

Did I believe we'd be better off without loud singing?

Did I believe friends should be left alone?

Did I believe that being related to someone made that person better?

Or worse,

What did I have against children?

Did I once think it a good thing to be anti-Moslem? Since Islam was, I once was sure, a violent religion?

But unlike the people I came from I was certain I did not hate

Jews or blacks or even supposedly, or clearly, ignorant local people.

But I had an unplanned technique for handling

The wrong people.

Men and sometimes women who might be homosexual

People who made me wonder about myself

Possible or for-certain Republicans

Some but not all relations

People who liked places I had rejected

Florida especially

Or people in wrong institutions such as Florida colleges.

Or worse, such as Princeton

Or people who were too religious.

I had handled it by pretending to myself that they either were

Not in front of me, or had stopped existing

These people who,

In their various ways,

Simply were not right.

FORWARD MOTION

I am too old to be a really good ukulele player.

That's not the only thing I am too old for.

I am too old to start again

Maybe

But not too old to care

Maybe

Yet too old to fill a house

With dogs and cats

I wish

Too old for new girlfriend in the singular or the plural

Too old for old girlfriends too

If not for serious remembered temptation.

Too old to go back in college years

To something more interesting

And I don't mean Yale.

But those small liberal places

On a planet far from the ivy ethos

But maybe I could play a ukulele anyway

And maybe my mind is good enough for sex

And maybe I will come to see

Things way behind rainbows

And ukuleles if not girlfriends

And behind the best dogs

And the cats I am now

Liking just as much

Even if cats are not dogs.

WITH OR WITHOUT

Softness with small animals

And behind small animals

Shot small creatures — what was it

What was it I shot and killed outside the building we called the barn?

He was dead dead dead

Will I know? Did I know?

Chipmunk hit with a .22.

Maybe this would be the biggest thing I experienced

Waiting already on a commuter train for the weekend in Greenwich

This death

Why always death in the air

Victims of Capt. Marvel and Superman

Spider Man.

Supergirl

Death was in the air

My reading

I had my hands on a .22 caliber pistol which belonged to a boy named "Sweaty." In this time that for the first time I was "Speedy"

This kind of beauty

in my arms

along the way

along my way

Along my way

Thinking of me

I wasn't swimming this time I was flying

To places where people got killed.

What I knew did not connect with

Connected a little… and not with anyone else

I chalking up hack books with some really good moments in them

I understood writing books alone so much like being alone with my mind
though pushing things different

ways.

Alone with my mind

Make it public

I am all alone with my mind

My mind, too, is lonely

To the observer:

I not writing…. Now I write.

My day was over before it could begin. What a waste!

When this chipmunk killed with a .22 shot gone astray. I don't know if it
went astray. Maybe I should know.

Can I go away?

I can't find and still can't find, and afterwards it will be I can't find.

Still there.

Or is it here?

Guns if not hunting

Very sharp knives for skinning.

BILLOWING REDNESS

I would like to go
down with the
Things
I want to sow or show
I want to move back
To where it began.
Unable to start at the beginning
And why not?
And do I care?
Is caring my problem?
On days when not caring
Can seem just fine.
The clouds today:
Billowing redness.
While I am imprisoned
In something less than a rehab
But more than an actual prison
I want to go where no one has gone before
Not parents, grandparents, twin brother
No one at all
Which I would say
If family were everything.

Facsimiles of paintings I love

Here in what I do not want to call my room

Billowing redness

Here over lawn in sweeping green

Here alone in my head

Is it lonely in my head?

Can it be?

What color is it inside?

This head of mine

A woman outside my room

Is ranting in senseless ways

And I want to be there with her

As she complains.

LOVE POEM IN HOT AUGUST

After you are gone
Long tree shadows
Over seething lawns
Seen through my window
While in too cold A/C
I play tunes
On my ukulele
After you are gone.
I still here.
Not in an old folks home
Not a nursing home
Just needed rehabilitation.
And through my window
Greenery was framing you.
Also an oblong bush
With faded reddish bloom
And growing out of the bush
Solid green sprouts
That look like they started
From virgin earth
I am so absorbed in color
And shape that
I forget buildings I see.
Past the sweep of lawns
I see a low brick place
Promising help to the sick and injured
A new more graceful building
Promises

"Adult day care"

But with you gone

Now more yellow

With remastered tiger light

In the full flowers

Contained

Above an oblong bush

A vertical sprout of faded light red

The sprout coming right out of the bush

And also straight from

Unplanted earth

Beneath a sky that does not divide

I do not see creatures

Any more than I see you

But I do see these growing things

Not the same as when you were here.

OLD TIMES AND YOUNG TIMES

The question was not did I hate old people?

Before I left in the morning we got into the bathtub together.

I let her think this was something

She was introducing this non-French person to.

IN AND OUT

Beyond all this I keep busy with other things — from learning to play
a ukulele to putting together what I think are vivid accounts of things
I have experienced in worlds that I can get to this way but often
not available.

Death and how I see it.

What if I don't die now? Then what?

What if I should live? List of things to accomplish?

When I speak of things to accomplish do I mean stories that might turn
into a book?

Or paintings?

A point at which I could never shut up.

What a wonderful thing lists are:

Things to do.

Things done

In and out of dreams.

TODAY MY DIRGE

Now I lay me down to sleep
I pray the Lord my soul to keep
If I should die before I wake
I pray the Lord my soul to take
If I do die in this time
What is left from then till now
And if I don't, what can I do
With whatever time remains
Could I start to write a book or symphony?
Or build a roof or wall or ceiling?
Or learn the cello or how to sail?
If believing I will not
Have time to finish
Any of these things?
And if I do nothing at all
Will anybody ever again
Invite me to anything
In or out of my known time?
Before, after or in the middle.
Or anywhere at all.
Whether now or in between.
My death.

WROUGHT IRON FOR VISITORS

In company or alone the lawn looks so inviting here, a sweeping lawn that seems to go all the way to the woods. Mid-summer green in many shades and with an occasional tree that looks so important its race must have an important biological name. I have been here long enough to get discouraged if I am counting.

But I am held by this landscape that is more complex than it first seemed. The grass getting slightly darker and ever more intense, while the flowers scattered around have not changed color so much as they have faded.

In certain reaches of the great sprawling lawn there are romantic little stone places with facing wrought iron chairs for people visiting from the outside. Easy to miss them in the sweep of the lawn they are on.

But what is less impossible to miss is the wrought iron fence. It does not move but it becomes increasing visible and imposing as if it had indeed moved toward the viewer.

Decorative wrought iron is the sort of thing the Donald Trumps and many Social Register people and some Ivy Leaguers would find classy and also proof of their monied position in the world.

And now as if on a hidden schedule autumn shows signs of moving into gentle summer and the air thickens. And the wrought iron bars seem blacker and bigger.

Till the point where it is the iron bars that dominate my landscape. Whether to keep the wrong people out or the right people in. Or to deny speculating.

Yes, the rolling landscape outside my window is not so friendly as it first appeared. Where are the chipmunks? Where are the rabbits? But what to make of red berries suddenly appearing on botanical things I cannot name.

TALKING

I talk to myself

I was talking to myself long before there were words with meaning

Or anything else I did not understand

But found appealing.

Like words between the pictures in books

In Connecticut I dove underwater at Compo Beach. They said this was the water of the Long Island Sound, which was deep and had a faraway feel.

I pulled myself down toward the ocean bottom

Though this was forbidden to me

On the list of things they made for me

That I would never be able to do

Swimming underwater like learning to read

So just after defying them by diving and reading

I went from Frost to Keats to Wordsworth

Without a backward glance.

DOGS AND TWINS

In New Rochelle we had a bony brown dog named Herbert that nobody liked. He was always on the verge of doing something awful like biting someone in a doorway he controlled.

Biting now being an actual threat not a metaphor. If I had been a little older Herbert and I might have become allies. But that presupposed my slipping away from the family,

It presupposed my finding out who I was.

I want to see foxes, and oh please God at least one polar bear in the wild and somehow not get cold.

During the war Aunt Betsy, whose husband, they said, was killed in the RAF, sent to our family an Old English Sheepdog named Neville.

Neville became the key family member. He would pick Peter and me up from the school bus stop, on a hill which we thought was a quarter mile away.

Mr Fanton lived on the hill. He was always watching from the porch that circled his house.

A very New England house, we were told. And Mr. Fanton spoke with a very New England accent.

We all loved New England but with some suspicion there was something wrong with it, that it could make people objects of ridicule. Rural people who did not have jobs in the city.

I was told our house once had a circular porch but it was taken away before we moved in.

When we walked past his house Mr. Fanton in his New England accent always had the same unanswerable question for us, after saying goodbye to Neville.

"Hello boys, what did you learn in school today?"

WHERE I CAME IN

Everyone I know and everyone I don't know,
Including all I know on Facebook,
They tend to say their families are their most favorite people,
As if no one has ever heard of parental cruelty and cheating
And this reminds me of where I came in
When the best thing most radio commentators
Had to say about a lay or political figure
Was that that person was NOT a Communist
While civilized people in circles I hit now
Do not put down Socialists
And on good days stand up to Fascists
Though some I know do refuse to go beyond family.
But others link to bad old ways
Even from the days of blacks called niggers
And Jews kikes
But oh God music
From Haydn and all the way forward
And also all the way back
And museums full of paintings
And oh God how I stepped out
Into Keats and Wordsworth.
And saw what my life could be
But there came a time
When getting the goods on families
Went to the top of my latest lists
Lists to put all things in their place

And keep them there,
And oh the cleansing anger
And oh the secret life
The secret
Of masturbation for example
And of the looming presence of
Hate and cruelty
And eventually
Betrayal.
I heard drums and went to play drums
in our 8th grade band
The drum section being for the bad boys.
I wanted to learn from dirty books
And I did neck a little in our movie theater
And planned to live in non-family places.
Which is why I lived all over the world.

THE POSSIBILITIES

In the dark
All the possibilities appear
And some get acted upon.
It came on wings of night
Coming through the rye
Hearts of desire
Fields of rye
Bowing
Or pining.
Sideways
Backwards
Bowing, pining
In a rowboat
In chipped paint
The water comes up
If not over.
I look to my shoes
A little cow shit
Rocks and mud
In and on the banks of
The Saugatuck River
Which I see with
My own eyes
The Saugatuck River my road
To adventure.

A DANCING PLACE

My brother before he died was back where he'd started
Not in far off places
But in the far north of home.
Trying to revive a dancing place in New Hampshire
The Playhouse where we'd met girls at early dances
The Playhouse on my grandparents' property
For social functions to make them and us love home
And wonder what might happen there.
Almost the way the world should be
But I wondered about dead animals
And my father's polio
And state-run executions
And what happened with the Jewish people
That they turned away.
And I became obsessed with blindness
Though I had perfect eyesight
And it was my brother, not me,
Who had to wear glasses.

PETS?

I want to go where mothers are mums and there are no questions
    about pets.

And live where greyhound racing is never allowed,

And neither is boxing

And football is marginal

And I never forget summer camps for the worst bullying

In the land of the free and the home of the brave.

VERSIONS OF SORRY

And always
Those empty-face people in wheelchairs
Look at those empty wheelchair faces
Those faces of what are called residents
A term that might seem caring
And a reminder that many will not
Leave this place alive.
Just now right here the head nurse confirmed
What I figured out.
Which is that current plans are for me to never leave this place
And never again have a cat that is my cat
Whom I love and who loves me.
I wait for my tears
Though quite certain I may never again
See tears that are mine.
I am that old and sorry.

RAVENS

But out in the sweeping still green field,

(Did I remember to say the field was sweeping?)

(And that it was still green?)

What seemed to be a rabbit

Seemed to be escaping into the woods beyond

While three big black birds

Came down all at once

All at once but not in unison.

I should add that I saw the birds as ravens

Though I had never seen a raven

I did know rabbits

But this one got to the woods first.

Did I remember to say the grass was still green,

Now and when my life was short?

NO MORE KLEENEX

So I look around this place where the head nurse (the ultimate person) says there is almost no dementia here.

I see mainly demented people.

One of them singing over and over a song that I cannot stand that was washed out when it annoyed me in childhood.

A dazed man is pointing out over and over that he has no more Kleenex.

Two other inhabitants are arguing about something which may be something I could write about. But I just do not understand what either of them is saying.

They are sitting out in a brighter lit place where most of the people eat their lunch. A mostly barren place called "The Day Room."

A previously unknown woman in The Day Room is calling and wailing for help. Most people in here are women which may be why they are alive.

"Help me. Please help me. Help!"

"Won't somebody help me?"

"Please!"

Nobody pays any attention.

This place where people in their demented ways may seem at home.

On the doors of many of the rooms are signs that say HOME SWEET HOME.

A few God Bless America signs are outnumbered by the Home Sweet Home signs.

Help! Help me please!

Is it insulting to say "these people?" It probably is.

Though I have what are sometimes called "the best of intentions."

Now a voice filling the Day Room again: "Help me to get home. Help me please."

"Will you help me to get home?"

NOT SPEAKING

Lethargy?

Is there a beginning to start with?

Does it have to do with lethargy?

Or with my demolishing early outcomes by becoming a champion debater.

Or my decision — that had the feel of inevitability — to go ahead without preparation?

Which felt like I had no choice,

Like my going to a college that seemed dead wrong before I started. Where the flashy F.Scott Fitzgerald had gone and my unflashy

father and grandfather too.

Which made me think of the many times I had been actually unable to speak. From way back when I went through stretches as a constantly frightened child, and again in the summer before I started college

A summer with the Experiment in International Living, which even Sylvia Plath was on, it was that upper class.

My Experiment time was in Holland — though because of art I had seen there on a family summer I had wanted to go to France. Which I could have done after college began, the regular time, with only limited choices for people like me who wanted to get away as early as possible.

But in Holland I found it impossible to speak, something I had thought was all over after my debating and actual honors in prep school.

In my final competition I won everything up to the regional New England finals that I lost. I feared one of the reasons for my loss had to do with having done none of the reading.

It took the judge of the debate two hours of going through his notes to decide I was not the winner.

A DEAD MOTHER

Why not write an essay?

Overnight my world got strangely smaller. Or strangely larger.

In the room next to the one I am in an otherwise perfectly nice woman talks with her long dead mother. Especially when I am trying to sleep.

In the room across the hall a lady who apparently seemed sane last year does battle with her wheelchair.

AT LEAST ELEPHANTS

I want to see an elephant in this field
That stretches out from my window.
Or at least see a cow here.
Don't need dinosaurs or horses from Westerns
Nor two-headed anything
I am staying alive for reality
I believe in what is real
And an elephant and a cow
Would add to anything I do
Some day I shall end a testy conversation
With the one word "Indeed"
But that is not enough to put me
At the head of the world
Where I had hoped to be
On certain good days
What I really hoped was that
I would slide into new poetry as fine as Keats,
Keats not Keats-and-Shelley
As if that one is a single one word
That they can use in place of the "death"
That secretly appeals
Though not so much to me I hope
As my mind roams
Through earlier days: on early sands and sea,
One fine teacher in prep school
If none in college
Where I did not dig
Into my real world life

Though now I deal with many writers
And not for them or me
Courses that tell you
Just how to write.
I would have no trouble
Writing about an elephant
If I saw an elephant
Right here in the field.
I mean a live elephant
As alive as a live cow
Or pretty girl
Or girl who was alive
And they did not say was pretty.
A girl walking across my field.

MY HORROR LIST

People I see
Who are alone
And/or depressed
And/or demented
My being wrapped up
With nursing home issues
Takes up space in my mind
That I must clear for things of value.
Thinking Burma, Bangkok and Bali
To take myself to other times
And then the loneliness.
That is all around I see.
Leading to depression with debilitation
That is how it is supposed to be
Which leaves loneliness
Not quite at the top of my horror list
This list,
Not quite one step from depression
Where my greatest fears,
Are topped by the dementia
In people all around me.

I find it hard to write
The word dementia
Hard because of a nursing home
Hard because my twin brother Peter died of Alzheimer's
But I point out that
although we were twins
we did not even look like brothers.
I started pointing this out
long before we were old.
I hope it stays this way in death.

CREATURES

This ominous sweeping lawn outside my window stays green while all around is death.

Sometimes there are creatures out there — wild turkeys, wild geese — and also a lone fox — but they are not out today except very briefly an identified black creature that is the same size as a turkey or goose but clearly is neither.

The black creature was inspecting the Christmas tree farm. What an idea, farming something meant to make everything seem just fine.

Fred Poole has lived a life of high adventure and art with some thorough delving into theology and matters of the spirit. In a past life he was the author of the novel *Where Dragons Dwell* and the co-author of the political exposé *Revolution in the Philippines.* In 1993 Fred created the Authentic Writing workshops, an enterprise that continues to thrive, supporting all those who want to write and get at their own story. Most recently, he published *Authentic Writing: A Memoir on Creating Memoir* and *The Aqua Mustang*, which takes on the enemy called "depression." He is a longstanding member of the Hudson Valley poetry community, and Calling All Poets in particular.

CPSIA information can be obtained
at www.ICGtesting.com
Printed in the USA
BVHW081556100722
641545BV00002B/100

9 780997 325867